The Coquí and The Iguana

By Alidis Vicente

Illustrated by Nancy Cote

The Coquí and The Iguana

Written by Alidis Vicente

Illustrated by Nancy Cote

Published by
Operation Outreach-USA Press
Holliston, MA

ISBN 978-0-9792144-7-9

Printed in the United States of America

FSC
www.fsc.org

MIX
Paper from
responsible sources
FSC® C103525

For Joaquín,
Who is always shining, and for any child in need of a little light in their life.

A.V.

In Memory of Ryan Kelly
Who loved Laz.

N.C.

My adventure began during a family trip in Puerto Rico to visit our relatives. I got to spend time with my cousin Sebastian. I had lots of primos living on the island, but out of all the cousins, he was my favorite.

1

We always played together under the palm trees while chasing little lizards around. I liked everything about the outdoors...except getting bit by mosquitoes. That part wasn't much fun.

2

So you can imagine how nervous I was when our family said we would be taking a nighttime boat trip. Mosquitoes love to come out at night, and there are lots of insects in Puerto Rico... LOTS!

3

"Don't worry, prima," said Sebastian. "La Parguera is a really cool place! You're going to love it!"
I wasn't so sure.

When we got on the boat, it was completely dark outside. The clouds covered the moon and stars. There were no lights anywhere. All I could hear were strange animal noises unlike any I usually hear at home.

5

Were they the hisses of giant snakes? Or maybe even the secret language of some strange bay monster! There was no way to tell.

"Maybe this isn't such a good idea," I said to Sebastian. Before I could convince my family to leave, the boat set sail.

The only animal sound I knew was the nightly chant of the coquí. I never understood how such a tiny tree frog could sing so loudly.
No matter how strong their voices were, I doubted a coquí could defend me against a team of snakes and bay monsters.

8

9

This place was beginning to seem creepy. I made sure I
sat very close to my cousin…just in case.

11

I was starting to think he was wrong about this place.
What could I possibly love about being in the middle
of a dark bay surrounded by mysterious creatures?
Then, he took out his flashlight.
"Watch this," he said. Sebastian quickly flickered light
on all the trees surrounding the boat as it crept quietly
through the water.

12

What I saw was awesome!
There were huge trees all around us!

I could see their roots twisting and turning as they crawled above the ground before disappearing into the water. There were even bats, snakes, and iguanas lying on the branches!

15

"I didn't know iguanas sleep in trees!" I exclaimed. "Not so loud!" Sebastian whispered. "We don't want to bother the animals. The coquís are singing the iguanas to sleep."

"The coquís don't put them to sleep, Sebastian," I said.
"Coquís just like to sing in the dark."
That's when my primo told me the story of the
Coquí and The Iguana. It went something like this...

During an especially dark, hot summer night, the sun
went to sleep on the horizon of the sea.

19

The moon, la luna, was taking a nap behind some very big clouds. Down below, the bay of La Parguera rested, surrounded by the long and winding branches of the mangroves.

21

On one of those branches lay an Iguana. The Iguana had eaten too much fruit for dinner and was falling asleep, listening to the song of a Coquí fill the dark air. "Coquí! Coquí!" it whistled. It was the most peaceful melody the Iguana had ever heard.

23

Suddenly, the singing stopped.
The Iguana woke up to listen closely.
It was of no use. The Coquí went silent.

The Iguana looked for the Coquí,
but it was so dark he couldn't see him.
"Coquí? Coquí, where are you?
Why have you stopped singing?"

"I'm over here," whispered the Coquí from a nearby branch. "I'm scared of the dark. I know I shouldn't be, because coquís only sing at night. But la luna is my night light, and she has gone away. I can't sing without her."

28

The Iguana had a plan. "Don't worry, Coquí. I can't make la luna come out, but I can get a night light for you."

29

30

The Iguana went down to the edge of the bay water and wiggled his tail. Magically, the water began to glow with all different colors!
The Iguana asked the fish to dance together to make the light shine even brighter.

33

"Thank you, Iguana! How did you do that?" asked Coquí.
"Coquí, even in the darkest places there is always light.
This is some of the most special water in the world.
It is a perfect place for us. You have no reason to be
afraid here."

35

So, the Coquí sang the night away without any fear as the Iguana fell sound asleep.

After Sebastian told me the story,
he filled a bucket with water from
La Parguera. I dipped my hand in.
The water began to glow, just like in the story!
I couldn't believe it!

38

"If a tiny coquí uses this as a night light, why can't I?" I wondered. Suddenly, it wasn't as dark anymore and all the mosquitoes buzzing around me weren't such a big deal.

39

40

To this day, when you visit the bay at night, the water will explode with color. And if you listen really closely, you'll hear the Coquí singing a lullaby to the Iguana...and to you.

41